*Leaf Graffiti*

Lucy Burnett was born in Dumfries in 1975 working in environmental campaigning, for many years before moving to the Manchester area. For three years she taught creative writing as a Graduate Teaching Assistant at the University of Salford while completing a Creative Writing PhD in ecopoetics, before returning to Scotland to take up a position as Creative Writing Teaching Fellow at the University of Strathclyde.

LUCY BURNETT

# *Leaf Graffiti*

*Northern House*

**CARCANET**

# Acknowledgements

Some of the poems collected in this book were previously published in *Chroma*, *Green Letters*, *nthposition*, *Poetry Wales*, *Presence*, *Shadowtrain*, *Stand* and *textyle*.

First published in Great Britain in 2013 by
Northern House
In association with Carcanet Press Limited
Alliance House
Cross Street
Manchester M2 7AQ

www.carcanet.co.uk

A CIP catalogue record for this book is available from the British Library

ISBN 978 1 84777 202 2

The publisher acknowledges financial assistance from Arts Council England

Supported by
**ARTS COUNCIL**
**ENGLAND**

Typeset by XL Publishing Services, Tiverton
Printed and bound in England by SRP Ltd, Exeter

# Contents

## I

## II

## III

# IV

# V

I

# Variations on an urban monotone

*an urban monotone*


i lay these words before your mind like bricks
   yet tentative   suggestive   as the way
a skein of geese is pointing   is mutating
in our autumn sky   our springtime sky
   this place is just a building site:   puddles
are malingering   the weeds repent
   cigarette butts fleck the clods of mud
     the scaffolds cordon off   and then the bricks
      which crumble into bits within my upturned
palm   wet clay remains clod up my hand
as my fingers web   and dry   to scattering sand
   windblown thoughts as white as hebridean
     you lay these bricks before my mind like words
      quite square   quite boxed   apartment blocked   i'm
teasing down the walls from inside out   the syntax
   capitals   full stops   i breathe   a pause
     that moment when we realise we're touching

*i. fungus*

grey flutters the grid of buildings amid the fungal
layers of dreich novembral cloud      a city
painted pale by their shadows    lacking chlorophyll
    spilling rain like the sweat of the city dwellers
        dressed in black    and white    and grey    absorbed
within the wheezing breaths of the urban mass
        a bus door sucking open    closed    inhaling
and exhaling    the emptied 7.30 crowd
    into the almost morning    caffeine wakened
crepuscules of labour    off to the tap
tap tap of the keyboard    computer breakfasts gulped
to the syncopated trills of the office till
    i slam the door to my tenemented stairwell
        stumble into daylight    my bicycle
wheels spinning clockwise    clockwork    running late
    and then i hear the sound    the monotonic
beat beat beat    of geese wings heading south


*ii. chlorophyll*

the sun has turned the people different shades
of green    their veins are chloroplasts    pumping
with the samba beats of summer    listless
lips are sipping on their chardonnay
    melon    kiwi    apple    tinge the wine
to green    olives spill their oil to grass
    unboxed neighbours mingle in the suburb
village square    a triangle whose apex
points towards the river    unpolluted
children green like algae    adults wilt
    the oak tree canopy that's shading them
survives another day unpatented
    as strengths of chlorophyllic blood are announced
in green    beech tree    willow    sycamore
    are pushing bicycles    and licking ice creams
from the deli    yet    as peppers ripen red
and olives black    the leaves    in turn    will turn

*iii. unboxed*

boxes stack untidily on top
of one another     outside the superstore
    half way up a mile long street     i'm found
alone inside the shop with twenty other
people     albinoed like my pansliced bread
    the wine i bought from the shop just down the road
        i'm semi skimmed     i'm over pasteurised
            my coppers count the contrasts on my palm
                one to thirty nine     i break the line
of coca cola light translated into
arabic     my offerings to this store
are aubergines and okra     coriander
    ginger     ghee        the voice behind the till
breaks into english just for me     we watch
the boxes stack untidily on top
of one another     take our turns     removing
from the middle of the jenga stack


*iv. milk*

i think a melody was born last night
at 3.15am     entangled in its
minor key     unlocking harmonies
    the melody is blind in 9:8 time
        i watch it growing visibly more painful
            semiquavers rushing to the silence
which i fear she woke to     memory
of the night before a solemn bassline
pushing through the curving tubes of the contra
bassoon     i guess she wishes for a visual
scar     a broken leg     some carcrash whiplash
    stitches from a fall     i did not know
that girl     walking home     around the corner
    yet tonight     she makes me dream of milk
        my mother's breasts     a nursery school bottle
            whiteness scattering my cereal
and my boxed in kitchen muffling out all sound

## v. whiplash

our lifestyle is a bit like whiplash    dancing
    cavorting    in a million cities    the world
over    tango    flamenco    ceilidh dances
    breakdancing    we do them equally
accompanied by cocktails    sherry    whisky
    beer    we entertain a million parties
        mingle with a many million strangers
wanting us tonight    last night    next year
    alone again within our tower blocks
        eight storey    six flat    social
extras' prisons    waiting in the lifts
    ascending    descending    well below
the basement level and up and off again
    apartements et casas    tenements
now terraces with different patterned streets
    fluorescent lighting beaming on a
million parties    dances needing danced


## vi. breakdancing

the dustbin men are spinning round the city
like a windmill    generating waste
        the wheelie bins are beergutted    obese
            spilling packagings    just like a gift
of unrequested feast    the dustbin men
will spin a marathon today    yet the seagulls
fatten    jostling for position    their squawking
beaks ajar    tongues flared    their outspread wings
hang sheer upon the open sky like puppets
    caricatures of poppy politicians
pinned upon the blue    a false remembrance
of tonight    tomorrow    you    it's true?
    the dustbin men are spinning round the city
generating waste    i watch it all
disintegrate    landfilled $CH_4$
to $CO_2$    and the popping and the piking
of the fluorescent yellow seagulls

*vii.  fluorescent*

by night we live as ions     four dimension
lowry figures    sculpted bright in stylised
black and white     our energy is charged
    is rigged    on liquid    pill    and powder halyards
        we are the evening's halo     a human painted
radius which elasticises out
between the suburbs and the centre     drawn
on dark    in light     a plane which circles up
above prepares for landing    watching    vulture
like     a flickering mass of luminescent
individuals in its sight     one by
one we dim     we taste the dawn in bovine
masticating bites     other halyards
clung upon and smoked     the day appears
too bright    our pupils blackening our eyes
        we're wearing evidence    bombardment    flight
        and what is left    is left    compelled    to write


*viii.  vulture*

our words must not become just carrion
    we shy the birds away with poetry
        vulcan like     watching over the ship
canal from penthouse flats    laptops on laps
    replacing gaps that industry once filled
        urban renewal fed by city foxes
            vulpine ticks of thought     deepening
in a city people cite as born again
    producing    reproducing    phallicscrapers
on the skyline    vulvalmakers of
a city park     perhaps in words     perhaps
we're *really* vulcans    (hypothetically)
    orbiting our myths of mercury
        messengers upon a messenger
            modern muses scripting atheistic
odes    vulgar vows    pre / post
modernity    vulcanising language

*ix. messenger*

the writing sprayed upon the wall is simply
enigmatic      whichever way i look
at it     an X     splayed lethargically
in black across the red brick tile effect
which is this tram line underpass      a fraud of
feeling trapped behind my retina
which lasts     as a snapshot stolen from a vandal's
purse     and all day long i'm speaking someone
else's words     my signature confuses
me     with me     a friend who calls my name
misinterprets me     identically
        i walk to work to unfamiliar hip hop
beats     arrive and meet my own relief
at the cross my colleague sucks between her teeth
     there is no question of belief     for she
is every bit as atheist as me
        if i crossed the road i'd confuse it for a kiss


*x. atheists*

we're maybe     all     more or less     the same
        variety packaged within a stereotype
             labelled up and never posted anywhere
else but here     wherever that might be
        for me that's here     just now     waiting for
the letterbox to flap     it's 4pm
on a sunday afternoon and i'm sprawled upon
the sofa watching football     texting all
my friends the goals     they're watching too at home
        their home     i wonder if they've had their sunday
dinner     text them     ask them     no they haven't
        funny that i haven't either and i'm
hungry     hungover     hung upon the sofa
like the telephone is slung upon its
cradle     badly     beyond engaged     the flapping
of the letterbox diverts me     smelling
pepperoni     mushrooms     mozzarella

*xi. mozzarella*

the countryside's been renneted     greenbelt
turned to urban curd     roads are named for
woodlands   moss   hedgerows   holly     coverts
covert in their lines of houses     lined by
credit cards and snorted up the nostrils
of the city     built within a shortlived
high of confidence for other people
      them     the not quite critically massed
            aeroplanes are taking off and landing
                  taking off to other     laden   city
suburbs     lines of houses seen from up
above as mozzarella     stretching from the
centre to many thousand open mouths
      while the vapour trails of aeroplanes are stretching
to many thousand opened cities     up
above the clouds in business class     they're relaxing
off their seatbelts     basking in the sunshine


*xii. critical mass*

i'm focusing on balance     we watch our own
horizons like a mirror profile     urban
skyline reaching ever closer     touching
on the glass we're looking through     a dozen
chimney pots     a leafless tree or two
      a terraced redbrick gable end     our window
views reflecting us     i'm focusing
on balance     our views hold steadier than the eyes
which fix upon it     flickering like moths
around a single candle light     we gaze
outside     a single plume of smoke surprises our
horizons     just as if i'm focusing
      on balance     it's held within the rise of a passing
blackbird wing     punctuated with
those freehand cirrus dashes and a neighbour's
wave     the poem crumbles over me
and into we     then out the open window

*xiii.  punctuation*

some sketch their skater vapour trails in violent
strokes     dashes     stops     punctuation
scratched in concrete slabs     underneath
the motorway     looping up above
their heads an arc     an arch     an archetype
        a road     the vapours of the constant car fumes
are ossified to bone     to stone     to concrete
        here the skaters hang     they meet     banished
from the street they skate to the traffic     droning
like bagpipe skies     no beat     but a bleat of the gambolled
ollie     the supervisor watches     chewing
on his seat     some low slung jeans     a beanie
        i skate my longboard down my suburban street
                weaving s's past the rows of neighbours'
cars     mercedes     escort     mini     saab
        i didn't see the pile of rotting leaves
                an eight year old shouts over     can't you do it


*xiv.  bones*

the rain has smudged the city sunday morning
        the winding curves of the multistorey car park
now look fluffy around the edges     i feel
an urge to hug it     yet i don't     i worry
what i'd do if i learnt it was only bones
        an empty rib cage     wrapping itself around
itself     enclosing spacious nothing     such
an empty word is nothing     not a word
you would embrace wholeheartedly     instead
i walk around the outside of the car park
        cars appear to enter     wait a while
            and then they leave     the cars are smudged as well
although they try and wipe it clear from side
to side     inside are people whom i cannot
see     tinted vague     yet one has left
her car     is walking now towards me     i know
her smudged and smiling face     embrace her bones

*xv.  tinted*

espresso aftertastes are playing on
my tongue    spitting dark brown clots of thoughts
    lavazza    cups in miniature    a pinkie
pointing 45 degrees at chimney
pots which rise above their gas effect
remote controlled    fires    a man is sitting
by a fire and reading newspapers
which take us to the city centre    party
conference and speeches    marches    protests
    everybody's words now hung within
quotation marks for nooses    clichés loosed
in headline bold    i fear we've gone beyond
the old yet still we breathe    the trodden air
is suffering our thoughts    and all that matters
ends right    now    i'll have another cup
of oxygen    *espresso* style    strike out
my broken crossword    yawn an O shaped yawn


*xvi.  oxygen*

i breathe the spider's web strings    tantalating
    titillising    silken strung    breeze
strummed    sprung with dewdrop bling    it's no
guitar    no banjo    more the torsioned pitch
of mandolin    which tunes itself upon
the crumbled corners where the window used
to sing    of promises behind    within
    a wasp is petrifying on a single
string    its wingless legless torso has been
mummified in swathes of motionless days
    yellow and black    merged to grey    it makes
me latinate    vespula vulgaris    prayers
drummed by raindrops slipping off the ivy
leaves which twist their living wreaths in green
    i only mourn the fact i cannot play you
        instead    i trace the lines upon my palm
            of hydrogen and oxygen and carbon

*xvii. bling*

gold hangs the necks of certain districts    betraying
us with better days    mocking with
medallions that have tarnished round the necks
of unknown others    leaving residues
of green    in these treelined streets    the weeds    whose roots
are ripping up the pavements    cracks down which
the neighbourhood  might not cave yet    though the worms
keep tempting us    keep promising    these necks
of gold we hang on certain districts    streets
are named for manors    colleges and kings
    who drive mercedes     wear their crest upon
their ring    in honour of the burnt out houses
    crack dens    brothels    bling    the neighbourhood
is fabric thin    we wear it    blithely trade
our ancestors for denim    t-shirts    tea towels    spring
    peering down the pavement crevices
the moles have eaten half the worms asleep


*xviii. crevice*

the morning crevices in monotones
    stammering upon its name    city
streetlight greyness shaken from the black
which wraps around us out beyond the ring road
    we are woken into mourning    drearied
into erstwhile photographs    void of
haemoglobin    chlorophyll    or saffron
   i regress    to uniforms and concrete
playgrounds    porridge    slate    it's all too late
    the lines of pairs of headlights strung along
the motorways    medusan dreadlocked    closing
in    i fear the moon's reflection turning
us to stone    while the bats have not danced
pipistrelles for weeks    the hedgehog has not
breathed for an hour    the dormouse body heat is
close to freezing    i'm condensating coffee
clouds in caves    and straw    and crevices

*xix. haemoglobin*

i don't know why we wear our brightest colours
on the inside      skinned in yawning shades of
white and grey and brown and black and yellow
      pumpkins     aubergines     courgettes     all pause
and laugh      we're merging with the dreary weather
      girning drizzle skull clouds     weary limbs
of aching blanket fog      a multicoloured
jumper and the vegetables erupt
      perhaps i might allow myself     that one
fine day along will come a surgeon or
a god or maybe just a change in weather
      take your pick     a penny or a pound
            and turn us inside out      wearing redness
proud as poppies     mullet     apples     kite
      the buildings will retreat away from crushing
cochineal      we'll feed on them like cacti
and we'll watch each other's hearts go <BOOM>


*xx. mullet*

the children on my street have gone and dropped
my poetry in candy      poems sherbet
dipped and chewed upon like liquorice
which stains your teeth quite chimney black but no
one really cares because we have to play
more cricket     mend a bicycle     and skip
along      it makes me try and write the world
in colour and to scale     but my street keeps
on turning up too big in terraced red
      britain too is crowding out      it's smudged
a commonwealth to mouldy green     it's spreading
      it's contagious     and the cricket ball
has landed in the grumpy neighbour's garden
      canada?      i leave my writing desk
and go out shopping      get a fish and buy
a haircut     interchangeably      the haircut
smells      the fish is an asymmetric mullet

*xxi. canada*

geese flutter the aerial view of urban tundra
       frost has blotted white the open parkland
spaces spurned by chestnuts    oak    or buildings
       roads      speckled grey as a canada goose
chest      the geese are spitting out their gaggled
space in rhyming fricatives    honking
counterpointed dissonance    a call
       an answer      their anserine duet    which swings
just like the way the see-saw in the playground
sings      today they shall not swim      their frozen
pond has cracked the sky's reflection    two
identical yet severed shades of blue
       and i'm split by memories too      my past
migrated through varieties of geese
              canadians mutate to barnacles
                     christmassing upon the solway too
                            welcome to scotland    we promise not to eat you


*xxii. barnacle*

geese flutter the aerial view of rural merse
       a wet december patchwork quilt of browns
and greens and browns and browns      my blotting paper
gathers up comparisons of sounds
       a flock of arctic birds    a rural concrete
playground      children praying that the bell
won't ring      the geese just holding out until
that moment when the cuckoo sings    of spring
       the barnacles are grazing on my past
              masticating moments which alone
could never last    to energy to re-
migrate      i bid the barnacles a V
goodbye    the weak will die    dropping plumb
lines from the sky      the rural dissipates
of late      again we scatter urban moulds
of living fungus    deadened bread    the canada
geese are pecking at each other's heads

*xxiii. patchwork*

the shopping bags are jostling for position
in the rainbow patchwork scarf which drapes
along the pavement    around the block    and back
    loosely knotted at its bus stop neck
          from time to time it flutters out across
the road      the doubledecker buses heckle
it with honks of horns      the bicycles
swish past    try not to catch it in their spokes
    the scarf is academic    so    we study
it    amo    amas    amat    the colours
do not go      red and orange    pink
and indigo      bulging to the brims
with presents    wrapping paper    food and clothes
    within a café just two streets ago
are twenty women sitting    knitting    drinking
tea and chatting politics    amo
    they knit one    purl one    knit one    purl one    knit


*xxiv. rainbow*

the fluorescent orange streetlights suffer
well the interloping neon coffee
cup    hanging pink above the entrance
to the bar      hanging us like placards
once hung drugs and meat and candlesticks
    we are the coffee    this is our cup    i sup
on it      girls are holding hands with girls
and boys are holding hands with boys    symmetrically
    and i'm licking on alliteration
          buy a bulmers at the bar    a look
of silent thank yous and a celtic tiger
sneeze    a thousand people cross themselves
yet no-one here believes    it's mid july
but it's very dark inside    outside it's getting
light    while i'm supping    gaily    on my cider
in these falling nights    masticating
bites    of apple    orange    olive    girls

*xxv. oranges*

'jesus is a lesbian upon
a beach in donegal'     the words i read
within the title on the screen within
the wall     i chew my cheek     it tastes of food
i think i'll eat next week     lemons     cherries
     kiwi     i'm sitting on an unplumbed toilet
seat     i cannot use the toilet paper
either     it's been written on you see
     and the words i read are     all     about     me
          i'm hanging round the art school scene just like
a writer     hanging on the cradle of
her girlfriend's arm quite badly     beyond engaged
     i think that i've materialised     been built
around in blocks of sandstone right angles which
face the pound shop littered city street
     there are lots of people i must meet     and lucky
me and i must go and drink a beer


*xxvi. cradle*

blue skies mock the mourning branches of
the oak tree without tears today     umbrella
timpani is silenced     a puddle on
the track beside the overtrellised gate
reflects a silver lining     and some rainbow
patterned seepage from adjacent streets
     red and yellow     blue and green     indigo
dulled to black     the oak limbs hanging burdened
from their cemetery back     no not
another bloody death it rustles     or so
the undertook assistant likely thinks
     idly smoking on his boss's blink
          the mourners sing     accompanied by torsioned
strings of spider silk thread violin
     hanging from some ivy     like you met
before     appeared once more     and a pair of swan
wing shadows overhead     and flying low

*xxvii.  timpani*

spray splutters the faces of the cycling
waterproofs along the former railway
line      individual raindrops drum
their multi-tonic timpani upon
the leaves      an a b c d e f minor
key      the concrete      and the bicycles
    the trees      we see the city skyline opening
up in front      it's pixellating me
with highrise flats      a castle      tenements
    volcano and the sea      we're simply the
periphery      we pedal round and round
our spinning wheels      weaving individual
patterns on the path      yet always forwards
    backwards      so      we reach our offices
        my desktop image tries to paint my day
more hebridean      turquoise      machaired      swept
        i drum out monotones      my snare drum desk


*xxviii.  machair*

the dogeared city seafront lies quite bare
    plastered garishly upon the shoreline
like some built graffiti      i am 'ere
it claims      the punctuation dropped      guttural
stopped in multi-coloured buildings      prouder
lime façades      the confessionals of old men
pubs and adolescent neon games
presented to the eastern winds with middle
finger raised      the waves recur      pushing
at the edges      nibbling at the shore where
beached up human layers are stratified
    ages straggled from the sea like seaweed
        generations textured like the mud
through sand      the concrete promenade we graze
upon like urban machair      some seagulls swoop
upon a fallen ice cream      excess chips
    some teenagers stub out their cigarettes

*xxix.  confessional*

i amble streets     kicking autumn leaves
        it's me     relieved by these volcanic shades
of umber        their dense december dampness cleaves
out grooves between my hooves and sticks like toffee
in my teeth        you know     i might not really
breathe        i kick the corpses of the leaves
        remember how they photosynthesised
            on me        like trees might wear their bark i wear
a coat of winter haar        draping through
the city street a scarf of sea     of me
        i kick the rotting leaves     feel the tarmac
pavement decomposing through the remnants
of my sleep        each step i kick is treading
on a different limb        an earthworm split
in half has severed me        i dig my chaetae
anchors in the leaves and burrow deeper
        i am i     and that is my confession


*xxx.  volcano*

is this asthenospheric then        down through
the sanded floorboards     past the continental
crust and hanging from the mantelpiece
        we name this place     reflexively     caldera
            cauldron     and as for us     we must be slowly
                surely     melting        we are the magma and this
is our pot        bueno     it must be so        i'm found
alone inside the flat with twenty spaniards
        nationalised like tartan     thistles     bagpipes
            drinking whisky *cola* in an accent
andaluz in edimburgo        hola
        hallo        my offerings olivas from
the olivo     greek grown        the bruja stirs
her pot once more     we're sharing sounds like loch
        reloj     and bruja     *witch?*     i find myself
outside again        hail the shining orange
beacon of a taxi     a black cab

*xxxi.  whisky*

his arm is crooked remorsefully beneath
his winter coat with whisky as he smiles
hallo     he knows my name and says it once
    again     tasting sibilance upon his tongue
in a slur of falling syllables     his hand
outstretches far beyond his coat sleeves and
their tassled tweed effect     a crumpled anchor
binds the joint between his hand and wrist
    he grasps my palm     i let him kiss it once
        again     he staggers back outside     returns
            a landscape painting from the charity shop
is slung beyond his arms     tilted like
an unrequited invitation     i lay
it down beside his other gifts     the specs
    the beads     the etch-a-sketch which draws the creases
in his rubbled face     tonight he has
a roof above his head     i cannot sleep


*xxxii.  etch-a-sketch*

a sofa is reclining on the muddied
river bank beside the train station
    i think i'm throwing stones at it     but it's dark
in that orange blackened     i can see you way
    the way the traffic tail lights stretch and etch-
a-sketch along a bank     upon a lengthy
shutter speed     or if you cross your eyes
    the way an orange flashing lollipop
is telling traffic     slow     their headlights dimming
on us     one step white     the next step black
    adult shoe size lino     the way that sofa
bundled down the river all the way
to here     reclining on the muddied littered
bank beside the train station     with nowhere
else to go     the lights turn green     the headlights
fill     a plastic duck is sauntering
downstream towards me     smiling orangely

*xxxiii. lollipop*

the child with curlicues is sucking     stubborn
as an ornamental figurine
     staring blue as china eyes     clinging
upwards to her mother's idle hand
     her parachute     i pay my eighty pence please
to the driver     cobbled coppers drizzle
from my downturned palm     i grasp my buzzing
ticket and its whiteness paints me beige
     how strange the way i feel myself just standing
there and holding on     those china eyes
     i'm staring at us wheezing through the steamed up
streets     i tell myself she knows     i know
     the way my uprightness     my uptightness
lets go around the corners and i snatch
a smile     i want to make her laugh and stick
my tongue out at her     clown like     broken down
     she sticks her fingers up at me     a V


*xxxiv. parachute*

it's 3am within the factory yard
and a skinhead worker argues with her brick wall
supervisor over hygiene     quite
predictably she loses and returns
to work     a hairnet on her scalp
for beating up the broccoli     as is her job
     her broom beats downwards     down upon her brow
          the supervisor     back within his office
blows upon his chillied hands     flicks
the kettle switch before his head submits
to gravity     his snoring wakes him up
     the quality control are smoking dope
and analysing stalks     they're far too long
     who cares     they idly pass the problem down
the line and no one feels aggrieved     least me
     i raise my skinhead to my parachute
          at least the sky     at least the stars     the moon

## xxxv. broccoli

from how it might appear    i might be writing
poetry    i fear    and researching
a vegetable    the broccoli    i'm flicking
through the entries in my dictionary
and tearing out our definitions    tearing
out the leaves    i tear it free of us
    of me    yet wear the florets round my neck
        objectively believe    my window's open
            cheers announce the scoreline in the match
just down the road    the greens are winning 1–0
    2–0    3    environmentalists
march issues through the city centre streets
    the presbyterian kirk bells dong the hour
to preach    believe    and me?    i pray of course
on broccoli    i'm tearing out the stalks
    the crux within the leaves    that broccoli
is just a type of brassica    you see


## xxxvi. presbyterian

the slush seeps like porridged brain    my fingers
filter through the gravel    leaves    the sweetie
wrappers and the grease and leave me melting
purity    it's dripping    dripping    and
my feet are getting wet    not yet i pray
    it's hardly sunny    shining like its shadow
through the mourning clouds    some teenagers
are shouting snowball battle cries    ice bombs
shatter windows of the cars which line
the cobbled street    diminishing to footfall
in retreat    yes the snow had fallen on
the night like grace notes    granted down from clouds
above    but it's almost christmas now    and carol
singers jostle with the shopping bags
which strangle through the littered city streets
    and this is how it's meant to be    relieved
        the snow had fallen just like human ashes

*xxxvii.  ashes*

i haven't seen an animal for four
whole poems    four whole weeks      perhaps we ought
to call it coffin syndrome      human boxed
    my eyelids have been closed yet still i blindly
watch      the mouldy walls are closing in
and even spiders daren't show their webs
    the worms retrace their paths    away    erase
their treads    and the sodden clouds rescind our shadows
    yes    the sodden clouds rescind our past
        until all that's left is centuries of human
ash      it's running through our hands like timer
sand    fertilising futures    undrawn
lands    i haven't seen an animal
for four whole poems    four whole weeks    as i filter
through my ash for moles or hedgehogs    dormice
    bats    i recall    at last    the moles
have eaten half the worms    the dormouse sleeps


*xxxviii.  shadow*

black flickers the city's shadow    the place we live
    reflected on our bricks and mortar canvas
we're simply stucco    stuccoed    stuck upon
some variations on a monotone
    background voices echo bagpipe drones
        *just* so    we *do it*    mocking our daily business
            shadows passing through each other    back
and past    as visual echoes of the last
    if we form a queue of mes and yous    the olds
        the youths    i wouldn't sue    i'm counting out
my overdraft upon my palm    its routine
shade of red    sanguinely dead    this *side*
*of life* the bank clerk shakes his brylcreemed head
    the other waiting clients mortgage me
        *the future's bright* a billboard promises
            of course it is    for sure    *we're loving it*
                i reach my hand to touch it    pass straight through

28

*xxxix. brylcreem*

so smooth as runny caramel    the way
the river creeps to sea upon a bag
of frozen peas    unless   instead   the river
was the destiny    the sea that crept
    so slick as 1950s peanuts    how
he flicks his rubbish from his car    confettied
verge now serenaded by the vroom
like way his cigarette-exhaust fumes merge
    so shiny as a chevrolet    the way
the packagings play rainbow in their freezer
hearse    haggling space    products bickering
in different styles of rhyming slogan verse
    so false as smooth   as slick   as shiny   how
the advertising moguls think of peas
    they speak american with jingo-ease
        confused upon a severed sea    oh how
my cities want to build on you in words


*xl. chevrolet*

sideways on and slanted    caught upon
an angle of a hip    a single label
and a frayless   always frayless   rip
    a useless pocket and an opening up
to nowhere zip    that catch upon my eye
like velcro   so   i follow it    i follow
    it?    the pitted pattern of heels
upon the pavement    the swagger in a sway
    the way it moves    grooves out future déjà
vu's along the passing looks that look
    like   me    i'm seeing me in stubbled
faces    hearing me in workmen whistles
    tasting me like bile in the underage
of a teenage drinker's throat    a lager gloat
    as i'm feeling me in the tailored suits which pass
too close    brushed to sheen    perhaps   on her?
    please turn and talk    is all   i ask   myself

*xli.  déjà vu*

strewth     the aubergines     within their lightly
lime sprayed satay sauce are merging with
another terracotta wall     clients
print evolving patterns     wallpaper
osmosing back to human form     the chef
is wearing     proud     his chequered trouser past
    the waiters polish their reflections in
the glass     welcome to this house of mild
narcotics     aubergines     potatoes     ties
and suits are huddled round their laptop world
    figures whirl and eddy on the screen
as a tie returns     warmly shivers     tobacco
breath as bitter as an outcast     cast
    he reassumes his role of sipping on
his bottled water     sparkling     french     while the other
two spin patterns     their starch white collars circling
round the remnants of their face-like plates


*xlii.  narcotic*

a siren bullies down the rushhour street
    setting sail to seagulls in the park
        it's getting dark although an early wind
is rustling up the newborn leaves     the litter
hastens down the road     while the limegreen copper
beech is previewing the fears of storm
the television forecasts later on
    the former hospital is boarded up
with hustings for developers     designer
flats     the cranes lift out its history
to dry upon the moon     this place is slow dance
death     i'm walking on the graveyard from
the plague     and my feet are getting wet     a passing
pushchair screams as if the child inside
suspects this triangle     her birth     my life
    their death     i gently stroke the longest side
        it slaps me on a gust of rising breeze

*xliii. triangle*

i'm spread out in a triangle      three cities
linked beneath those selfsame fungal layers
of dreich novembral cloud   you know    i'm almost
equilateral      pointing three
directions like a faulty compass      i am
my own magnetic variation      i have
my own direction      my needle spinning from
an early rural home    as some dewdrops on
the grass combine    reform    in city rivers
    ship canals    a seafront promenade
        i toss a pebble    wait and watch the puddle's
ripples    circling out like treetrunk years
migrating      if i reach this high i'll milk the raindrops
from the autumn sky    drop them on
the roads and houses    parks and office blocks
of these three cities    these three streets of leaves
        can you smell the moss    the conkers    rotting bracken


*xliv. fungus*

the frost will script the morning      crystallising
on my windows will be frozen dances
of the dandelion parachutes
        the sky will startle into blue    anew
            i'll open the door to my tenemented stairwell
                stumble into daylight    running late
                    my bicycle wheels spinning clockwise    just like
clockwork    then i'll stop    will hear    will watch
    the beat beat beat    of geese wings heading north
        re-loosening my barnacles from rocks
            fluttered Vs which mock us and reform
to mock themselves    an us and them to us
and us      i'll watch commuters emptying
the bus    continuous as cells of fungus
    these variations on a single poem
        photosynthesis    of monotone
            and the pounding of the geese wings pulsing home

i lay these words before your mind like bricks
    yet incremental   slanted   the way a skein
of geese shift wingbeats south or north   without
a loss of autumn into springtime skies
        this place becomes a building site   puddles
slick with rainbows   dandelions bloom
    cigarette butts pebbledash the mud
as the scaffolds cordon blocks of colour off
the sky    and then the bricks   which crumble back
from bits within my upturned palm   windblown
thoughts as white as hebridean   wet
from sand   to clay   are clodding up my hands
    you lay these shapes before my mind like words
      unsquare?  unboxed?   these tonal building blocks
as syntax locked   from outside in   to this.
    Punctuating breaths, an empty pause.
      Exhaling, we suspend our sense of touching.

II

## Inheritance

A dried out lemon
on a dusty desk –
all the thoughts
of all the words
unwritten.

# Bark

*Westland, New Zealand*

Just a micro segment captured singly
in macro form. A moment stopped,
stilled, blink and miss it, blink of lens
and snatch it now, forever.

I stole back nature's moment, chemically.
Burning, dodging, counting darkened minutes
of a process stopped and fixed.

Time recapitulated, images reviewed:
they were rotting brown and orange flames
glistening moist as stricken lava

stilled: so did I shoot the centre of the earth?

Radiating out a roadside heap of red wood
trunks have been abandoned,
left to mites to crawl and creep designs.
Eight-foot ferns fan overhead, condescending,
mocking; unseen birds all gather round,
and glacial rivers flow cloudy back up-stream to re-ice.

I dreamt about Aoraki as eclipse.
Everest is tilted off upon an angle, drooping low.
Our maps have been redrawn and oceans stilled:

my home a micro zig-zag, stuck upon the edge
of afterthought.

## The homing nomad

'where are you from?'
you ask

*cross the border, turn*
*left, and just keep going*

i reply

my unfurled smile
deepening the furrows
in the contours of your brow

my home was a dot of dust
my home was getting warmer

my home was the space
the homing pigeons knew
by undrawn heart

# *River    just*

the butterfly was just another floating
dandelion dancing up and down the river bank

   fluttered yellow    luminously sprung against
the april grasses    green    i wanted only words

you know    just like the butterfly    that floated dandelion
dancing up and down the river bank so soundlessly

   a passing couple held a conversation in a
monotone behind my head    illegible against the blue

   and you    returned    i could not say a word    but watched
that dandelion    floating like a butterfly    sprung

## Oliva olivo

she sits quite still
a single olive in her hands

her stare which catches
on the hairs of my upturned
labourer's neck

the hills of cadiz
are weighed with fruit
and the altered rhythm
of a waning autumn sun

our choice reduced
to which tree next

'pero estoy mirando a ti'

oliva, female, fruit,
olivo, male, the tree

an uncertain gift
declined so simply

take this letter A

# Oval

## i. the consultation

The rubber gloves were outlined in a single word;
no freehand glimpse, a blackened felt-tip border, sure,
precise, holding in their milky vagueness just
above his right hand shoulder, white on light, on white.

His voice seemed slurred, like hearing under water,
schwas of sounds, one word and rubber gloves that held
their germs within and washed me cold at twenty one
degrees. A dettol touch of facts and probabilities

were interspersed with quips about daytime tv shows,
banana smiles and jokes on ways to 'boost your chance
of living if the news is bad'. I felt the touch
of rubber down my spine, its pulling, catching stroke.

Outside I saw in gamma vision, children's book
of blues and greens and yellows. Shirking reds, I crossed
the road and cars slowed down but didn't beep their horns.
A single word was spreading everywhere today.

## ii. the invisible

The invisible is happening everywhere today –
today i see it clearly – self-aware machine of me.
I watch my breath as bloody streams of oxygen,
drowning life from inside out. Doubts appear
quite clear in neurone etch-a-sketch –
steroid hormones more than just a concept,
painting classes, body easel, model me, now
studying my songs in cycles, looped vibrations,
body halo, frequencies – the invisible is happening
everywhere today – today I see it clearly –
nanoseconds burst to life in technicolor flashes,
gravity appears in multi-tangled parachutes inverted

down, the solid ground a trembling myth, as the air
and water merge in waves which overlap on
everything we see. We are touching at the edges.
Separation into me. A needle or a knife.


*iii.  the separation*

I'm standing balanced on a stepping stone,
my ovaries are cradled in my hands.

I rock them gently, whisper words which float
like dandelion parachutes, carried
back to me in altered sounds of birdsong,
running water, silence of the hills.

Intertangled cirrus feathers stroke my
hair, the sunshine dapples me through newborn
leaves, the breeze is diffident, the air
is pungent with mitosis, time is blurred.

I free my clasp and, passive, watch one flow
downstream. Bumping, trundling, as a
single oval pebble smoothes its way to sea.


*iv.  the rain*

I thought myself the centre of the earth, then,
waiting by the full-length window, staring at the rain.
Years of science ditched, no need to travel seismic waves
through crust and mantle. Magnetic fields originated
there with me, leaning on the shoulder of a friend,
a haze of anaesthetic hangover, dripping at the edge
of consciousness, smudging borders around my musings
on the worst-case possibilities, scenarios and fears
of diagnosis. I watched the raindrop archipelagos
disintegrate upon the window panes, islands drowned.

No one would have guessed it in my isolated gaze,
yet activity was spiralling around me. Ambulances
wailed emergency, as I watched the automatic doors:
opening, closing, opening on a watercolour car park
filling up for visiting. A father rushed the multi-coloured
jackets of his children round the puddles from his car.
Beyond – the road – the daily mental illness of the rush hour
as my lift arrived. I timed my exit through the sliding doors
deliberately and splashed directly through the puddles.
Raindrops fell upon me like the arrows of a cold front,
pointing at me, reaching out to me, and coming near.

*v. the mirror*

I'm wearing no clothes. Right this minute, now,
my eyes averted down as though i am ashamed.
Centred in my parents' room – the door is shut –
a certain sign, a symbolic line of suture. My scar is
six inches long, its darkened, slightly crooked smile
which makes me tilt my head like nurses do.
I slowly stroke the bruises of my swollen side
as I try and figure if the dent I feel is really there.
My skin appears to droop and sag around my fingers
in contrast to the fullness that I felt before.
My fingers knead my new-found lack of symmetry,
a half-aborted womanhood. The doctor promised me
'the woman left will end up working twice as hard'.
I wonder, catch my own reflected eye, what if?

I wonder, catch my own reflected eye, what if
the woman left will end up working twice as hard?
'A half-aborted womanhood', the doctor promised me,
my fingers need my newfound lack of symmetry,
in contrast to the fullness that I felt before.
My skin appears to droop and sag around my fingers
as I try and figure if the dent I feel is really there.
I slowly stroke the bruises of my swollen side,
which makes me tilt my head like nurses do.
Six inches long, its darkened, slightly crooked smile

a certain sign, a symbolic line of suture. My scar is
centred in my parents' room – the door is shut –
my eyes averted down as though I am ashamed.
I'm wearing no clothes. Right this minute. Now.


*vi.  the lather*

It wasn't tangerine and fizzy sweets.
No euphoric bursts of blossom,
not a primal scream nor dewdrop tears.

I wore the phone call factual, cold,
my mother's smiling arms around
my shoulders felt like just another layer of clothes,
as the radio droned with background news:

paralysis had moved.

Inching out beyond my metricality,
as if I needed scientific proof –
a single atom rhyming with release.

The fingers of benignancy
are lathering my back
and wiping clean my body armour.

III

## *Visceral   impossibly so*

where the morning is    unsure
   no counterfeit of potency
but a hazing around the edges
where the sand might be    blowing
   near to an edge of sky
and falling granules into day
   exfoliating worry    sleep

   an overhang of petrol sky    sinks
through variously grey    a contour's texture
   visceral    impossibly so    a layer of rain
   its threat of an offering withdrawn
while the rush of a rising wave
approaching shore disintegrates
its shape upon itself    repeatedly

   leaving you with this    perhaps
a rainbow    a reaching sheen of water
over sand    a metallic tinge of salt to air
that worries with reality    ellipsed
   or the other scattered debris of
the sea    driftwood    fishing
crates    and a slick of dead birds

## The collared dove

wake up now

    peace arrives in a collar
of the woodland
   out of site

     if i see you it's cosmetic
       blueness branding
the jet streams

   we are out of words
but the sounds of morning
    subsongs opening copses

into silence

## *Walking the mud*

walking the mud
sailors call it

    checking the anchor
      checking the buoy
        checking the hull
          prising barnacles
with a blunt chisel

    the sink of mud between
my toes is somehow
comforting

    siphoning my legs
and knowing that the tide
will turn

      ...

    or walking to an island
      a beached whale

      calibrating meadows
        roughening of shingle
          decaying stakenet teeth
          prising barnacles
off its under flank

    the fossil stare of herons
and a final spurt of sky
    of butterfly

      imagining its rotting breaths
i finger shingle-whalebone
in my hands

## Otter's pool

splinters of tree ripple
reflect a shattering
twist of river

  you sit on a boulder
granite island    current divided
   are you waiting

    individual sunbeams
pierce a splice of fingers
   widening lower autumn

   you reach your hand
to touch it
   pass straight through

      there won't be otters here today
        no kites on the red kite trail
          your lover calls your name

out loud    removing
you    like the river's
severed limb    by limb

## Decidua

falling off from a beginning
    shedding first breaths
        we commence an end
            another season is offered
up to us to cast in words:
    late autumn light rusts
to umber    the curl of the
underskin of silver birch
    deciduous as parturition
        a transitory nightfall

## Acorn

let's grow    just like that oak tree
grows    both ways    both at once

     i hold an acorn in between
a finger and a thumb just like a bruise

   both ways    both at once    let's grow
just like that oak tree grows

    i hold a bruise between a finger
and a thumb just like an acorn

   let's slow    just like this moment
slows    both ways    both at once

## White space

unfolding into
compass bearings

there is no way
but further into
a white-out

counting every step
of disappearance

limbs of temporary
treads sink hesitations
erased
repeated

as bodies leaning
in and out of mountains
curve their skeletons
to contour lines
to isobars
embodied into white.

But mostly blizzards
interfere the silence
and the slowness of mist

# *Vapour*

next zig of swallow vapour trail
on a sky i filter to blue
   the loss of anemone kisses

# Flaxen

a lack of drama this defeat
   just broken subtraction
one from two    a single woman
statues    off-yellow the floor

   a cross of her legs a lotus
      or your unawareness caught
between your hand    and you
   as a ball of flax is cast

   unravelling strip
diagonals    imperfect
spheres    diminishing across
a length of studio

   direction hesitates
      deprecating an impact's
muted crumple    flaccid
   further to the floor

   you lift your hand
towards yourself and wear it
like a glove    a hang of linen
to your languid petal skin

   this woman of clay this
woman not of clay    or a mould
the colour of flax    a fray
of your thread of flower

## Yellowbells

somewhere is a place
i don't know yet and i'm
walking there

  my girlfriend clasps
my hand in hers and tells
me all about the flowers

  i'm not quite sure
about the bluebells
being yellow in disguise

but before we know it
we've arrived    a disappointment
quite so beautiful

  the sun is shining through
the dumpling clouds
and the daffodils are blue

  we name our destination
for the non-existent
fields of yellowbells

## *A rainbow will equivocate*

this nameless river
   pupil of an iris
raincloud

   no irrelevance nor
no pity as a rainbow
will equivocate

   pittance of a
summer is expounded
in a tideline

  unwaiting for
the autumn    winter
   spring    a swell

of fall    of ripple dance
   a moment's chance
that also lands us here

   no irrelevance nor
no pity as a rainbow
will equivocate

its end: out to sea
   namelessly    the pupil
of an iris raincloud

## Icicle

still unknown
   the hollow beat
of a dripping tap
solidifies its measure
   unseen time to ice
    a moment's
stalactite
   no handle on it

## This proximity ·

this november this proximity i might have i dreamt of this another
day that tangles beginning with itself between a continuity or break
no word like dawn no dusk for the ending of this night as the
nocturnal will retreat into another darkness lost bats hang like rotten
leaves upon forgotten eaves the nightshift clocks to the early pub
and just unseen and the moon retreats its slice of orb sloping
elsewhere for the opening out of lightness into day vague moments
the flickering dim of the headlights will suck the cats' eyes in alarms
will syncopate the rhythm of a staggered wake more vertical as the
sun suggests itself in the lightening of an eastern face all this
proximity vibrates potential day yet undecided

# *Heatwave*

heatwaves of pollution scatter the directions of a flock of poisoned fish
    one eyes to the sky    the yellowing smell as the fishes putrefy and
scales that melt into the sheen of a silvered sea

a chinese man is swimming though his dead farm    touching violence

# Counterpoint

the counterpoint of
a pair of barn owls
    unseen in darkness

       the echo of a single call
reflected in the syncopation
of the other's variation

    back and forth    and
back    their own proximity
offsets a distance

    but for whom?
       our footsteps crunch
upon the frosted track

and a bat composes silence
around our profiled clefs
    its sonar score of dips

and dives of musical notation
    an echolocated script
illegible as black on black

on an empty stave of sky
    our swinging limbs
must now dissolve to dark

in the metronomic beats
of arms    of feet
    and the measure    in the

holding    of our hands

# *Uncompletement*

*i.*

like these words
    forever fragments
        uncomplete
themselves once
more

        a single bud
of spring becomes
the first    no longer
        unfurling leafs
a slightest

variation    another
year to autumn
        ends recede to increments
and a single leaf
uncurves towards

*ii.*

like these words
    forever fragments
        uncomplete
themselves once
more

        a single bud
of spring becomes
the first    no longer
        unfurling leafs
a slightest

variation    other
constellations

              as angles shade through
greens     beyond
    another autumn

        ends recede to
increments of change
    and a single leaf
uncurves towards
this earth

        its crusted corners
carve out lines across
an early frost
    these serrated edges
        both potential     loss


*iii.*

like these words
    forever fragments
        uncomplete
themselves once
more

        our conversation
will elide
    sliding meanings
into silence
    the hang of it

            a single bud
of spring becomes
the first     no longer
    unfurling leafs
a slightest

variation     other
conversations
    our angles shading

greens    beyond
    another autumn

      ends recede to
increments of change
    and a single leaf
uncurves towards
this earth

    its crusted corners
carve out lines across
an early frost
    these serrated edges
      both potential    loss

      the release of
falling    soundlessness
    no speech of a leaf
    revolving on it

just turning    turning

## Green words on grass

green words on grass
        those jointed stems

            elongated sheaths
of leaves

    flowers in spikes
and seedlike fruits

    verdant verbs that
*tell on you*:

that globe of dew that
bubbles    mirrors

    bursts itself upon
a pointed tip

and slides to graze
        the way it's seen

            a lean of words
upon a single blade

of grass    a touch
of all but green

        a double edge
            a cut on me

IV

# Fountainbridge

'ADELE 19' is plastered
9 times over
on a billboard
by the broken brewery
in Fountainbridge

the bridge which used
to span the road
with beer with a clock
on it has gone now
so we're all out of time

but there never was
a time for fountains    here
only a namesake pub
which spouts with smoke
– or men in tracksuits –

smokescreens      this is
Dundee Street    not the way
towards dundee
so paint your trainers whiter
dance    it's Saturday night

## Hedging bets

if you walk that city street in august
you might feel the rise of sprinklers
watering the brittle hair of pensioners

    around here death is more than likely
not the talk of the blue rinses hobbling
down the road towards the psychiatric ward

    what to talk about      i'm walking down
the hill from a visit to an aunt who is not dead
and is not dying either     what else to do

    i place another black–jack chew upon
my tongue and stick it out to watch    dissolving
blackening    the purpled sugars trickling

down our throats like liquid smiles
    i'm running out of downhill now     the streetlife
levels and a mongrel pisses on a berberis

## Slabs of strawberry

*after Edwin Morgan*

i love a smoking glaswegian
strawberry in concrete

    mostly

as the juices of your words
trickle up my chin

extinguishing the draw
of us from the tips of
your ambidextrous cigarette

Presumed insomniacs drag feet along pavements lit by the irises of roadmen. Behind curtains snuffed where the wheels decelerate and the night becomes speed, following the trail of a cigarette for warmth or the smell of the levelling of tar. While television programmes tire of a drunken man on the back seat, downhill in the highest gear. Reaching beyond the end of the leash take a break for tea in the cab, spectacles removed upon the bedside table on top of this week's novel. For the sake of a single fare, choose to head out west. The dogs at night don't bark and there aren't many women among fluorescent vests. At the edges of the pillow the final passenger alights: throats catch on air, eyes water. Strangers don't seem to say hello as if they should. Still. The formless chatter of the workmen jerking movement towards sleep turns ignitions, faster darkening beyond the orange glow of streetlights into approaching, off. As near as this to black and faster still.

## *a fibINtwoacts: aflower*

T
h
eP
lan
tPotI
sMonisti
cButItDoesn't
HaveAClue. WhatToDo.
TheSunflowersAreBrokeN


.


Be
gin
Again
TheSeeds
AsParachutesO
fConcrete:Dioxidising

## Late sunday above the forth

lightning forked in two
    backlit    i missed it
      i start to kiss you
against only sky

     boats pass beneath
our feet where the
architects suspended us
    high tensile wires

stringing us to the storm
until the petrol clouds
diverge  −  tangential
to our lips:

    for i will go this way
as you turn that.

    the thunder echoes
      boats' wakes dissipate
        no more a walk
above the night    more

an unpreparatory sketch
    a neither here nor then
      the background blur
of the traffic's transit

    just passing by

## Innside

in the one-way street which place forgot     a felt-tip female profile
sketches west towards the open road     her frank brown-paper gaze
glued to the MDF of the former church inn     a bustless neck-up
bust and eyelashes you'd give your granny for     her collagen-
plumped pout is outlined black as marker pen     you'll only last six
weeks round here love     let alone the rain

it's sunset beyond the clouds and the cars are leaving us
     someone's pulled the aerial from the sky and the traffic hums
flat spectrals     white as raindrops drip the smudged bass     arterial

THIS IS A DANGEROUS BUILDING. DO NOT ENTER

a half-full coca cola can she didn't drink stands upright on the
double yellow lines of the cobbled street and a greenall's logo
trumpets beer two hundred years due east     lettering emptying into
space and silent lock-outs

ARSON IS A KILLER. ARE YOU?

the graffiti on the redeveloped red brick wall of the churchyard just
around the corner answers YES!     you walk me west against the
one-way street     towards the shalimar     buy news and booze and
cash (and more coke)     we're staying open late     across the road
the cathedral's western window consecrates its own date

*when I am lifted up I shall draw all men to myself:*
          please pray for anne for she is lost
          also pray for joe     who is less lost

## Footfall

writing found
beyond windows
   another day of rain

      a stream lightens
shades of brown
towards rivers

    i feel lighter
as a sense of loss

    no depth of trees
to silhouettes
and the flattening
of picket fence moss

   casting off dimensions

     sky becomes paper
without nuances
between greys
   raindrops
     hieroglyphs on glass

       perhaps we quit
the curfew
   and if we run before
we walk

   as light as light on streams
      lighter    losing

# Astrophysics

we were studying the physics
of the colours of the rainbow
in the statues found around town

    i counted fifty one but i might
have missed a couple near the ring-
road    passionately kissing

    i miss that time of night
where everything is as it is
    there are no question marks
to punctuate a dream

  just the separation of the rainbow
into frequencies and the speculation
of the angles where lovers meet

    knowledge idly unacquired
and a final statue cast in bronze
    its coldness to touch

## Herring boats

i had never thought
about the quality of
the housing stock

   nor pondered the
extravagance of the
concrete cantilevers
at the parliament

   as you flick the pages
of my city with your
architect's eyes of grit
   materialising form:

      *a gathering situation*
         *an amphitheatre*
   *coming out from arthur's seat*
      bright as the rings
of words we legislate
in stone.

   Seven upturned
herring boats are sailing
where the seagulls fly the storm
and the morning's catch
of fish is a net of leaves
   a gabion cage of quarry

# Sheeps

*i.*

If the singular of sheep is sheep,
collect them individually,
tick the pictures.

Cumbria as Herdwick,
Derbyshire as Gritstone,
Leicestershire is Blue.

Midlothian: a mammary gland
that died of lung cancer.
Pickle it, stuff it: exhibited.

Home has a black face
and is always moving.
Herd the mother sheep
and the rest will follow:
clone sonnets from wool.


*ii.*

In between homes, pulling ourselves
aside into a table and chairs where
limbs splice into limbs – table top tacky
from previous morning rounds –
we wear the menu willingly.

Butcher, baker, flower-maker:

*You could almost buy a sheep for
the price of one Moroccan skewer,
locally grown.*

But the lambs are getting older
as we drive due south, and the models
change. My accent shifts a little
every time we stop.

Shifts that take their toll
upon the mutability of genes.
Varying the sequences,
coding words for something else:
possibly formica as a verb.

We do not ask each other
for the answers, written on
the reverse. Which question?

A limb is a limb is a lamb.

*Pure bread.*


iii.

Home-kipppered, peppered, ragged, phrases taken
by a curious route. The state of us and the price of lamb.

Harassed by work, housing shortages, and ageing
prematurely. Our telomeres are too short.
We will die of cancer if we spend our lives indoors.
If arthritis sets in early – restore it thoughtfully –
a valentine of euthanasia

*We are going to get decked.*

It's not natural but the longer-lasting benefits
to the sonnet and the shape of wool;

*85 pence a kilo for the live meat. Fifty, sixty pounds
will buy a whole one, ready, freezer-dressed.*

If a short parenthetical remark is needed,
the question is a paraphrase. There is more

V

## Giving over into wings

Awake, and tingling near the air,
I write about the sun
as a place I know.

A collage of an afternoon –
the architecture of the mountains,
vanity and wax.

A splash of a mountain
stands on a hillock,
advertising all I write.

*I am Icarus*, I lie,
*a prisoner of flight.*

We eat the plums in any case
and head back home.

At night on a haybale by
the clouds, you told me all
about the antiseptic stars

Alfalfa, Spirulina, Barley grass

a rush of verbal calories,
a wing-shaped human
constellation gathering around
us into words.

At 4am the sun begins to rise
and we hold bare atoms on our arms.
Alteration of disturbance
at an average rate per year;
anti-heroes fissioning to light.

## Schiehallion

take the mass of a fairy against
the deflection of a woman's breast
    gravitational constant as storm

       the picts hid whales behind
the cone of a mountain
and framed the queen a view
    we saved the dog's mercury
       turned the lilies into valleys
and gave your name an oilfield
    *the mountains are calling*

*and i must go*
    the density of this earth
is a ceilidh reel and a brand of lager
    limestone is our pavement

      if latitude and longitude meet
where the pendulum clocks G
    we will walk from here

    contour lines are secondary

      if further centres
further into circles
    if the weight of the world
is a story cupped in cumulus

# Snowlight

Changes at peripheries of vision
slanted angles which I pin to my lapel
like steppe grass and some mountains for boots.

Inventing snow-light as a way of life?
the touch of feathering –

...

for mostly we are tramping on the roofs
of houses, hanging thoughts upon
the punctuation of the opened sky.

We scuff our heads through clouds
and sieve our raindrops out of dirt.

The wind feels louder than the sun
and our moods spin blueness from
grey, avoidance of another winter
or an even chance of summer snow.

We will fly higher through migration's
transitory sky – we'll touch the furthest sun.
So we turn the dials of our hypotheses just so
calibrated frequencies as altered skies

enforcing shedding
limbs of snow to life.

If I take it as a motion into weightlessness –

...

might I slide into the slip-streams
of migrating birds

returning home to Svalbard
where the summer permafrost
is blooming like Euphrates

there will be 99 days of midnight sun
and 84 of polar night
living life by the light of snow
and the turn of tides by moons.

There is no way back but sideways
a way of thinking into wings
destination otherwise.

The global seedbank of our lives
is buried in a vault cut deep
within the rock at minus 6 degrees

re-storing everything to nothing –

# The evolution of flight

So here I am, then –
the bird with no wings.

A keel-free sternum.
I could not have even flown
had I really wanted to.

The aeroplane ran out of sky
and set out for the moon.

*We were one small step.*
*We were a giant leap.*
We were walking on a form of air too thin for even breathing with.

When I got back home after a day out picking clouds
my eyes were as burnt as indigo suns and my feet fell off the balcony.

The spirits flew the pigeon into the Adriatic sea,
the lanterns scared the enemy and the hapless Berber lacked an
    aerodynamic tail.

The hotter sky has advanced our first and peak appearances by
    several days.
It was only a matter of time before we broke the barrier of sound.

icarus is depressed by the thought that,
after all, the hero may be another version
of himself, gone elsewhere

by the time that he had solved the mystery
of the disappearing sky he had disappeared
himself

> he empties his limbs into another
> glass of rye – what else to do when you've
> lost the plot line to your life?

his nightmares are armadas, fleets of
caricatures, pseudonyms, mongrel wings

the solar cycle which he sees reflected
in his drink is a scattered shade of green

> 'now,' he said, 'where was i?'

> the symbolists had already done away
> with polar bear and rising seas

> before he knew it they'd be abolishing
> the globe – as seen from space

after five whiskeys icarus was drunker
than the whiskey itself

'i might compare whiskey to helium,'
he said, 'it lowers the voice as helium
elevates balloons'

His soul was transported to the traveller,
who multiplied the earth by his imagination
with dreams of being guided by the wind

So let us swim!

When he reached the inner core of earth
his heart was a pickled onion, his skin was
hanging from his chin like a burst balloon
and his eyes were staring, shaking –

oneiric hard-boiled eggs

## Battery

I had a dream that someone stole my bicycle
and the rain was a petrol shade of blue.

I'd just come second in the tractor-pulling tournament
and the chickens watching from the sides were shrieking
like a battery of vuvuzelas. I couldn't shake the smell
of excrement, lingering like a memory I never asked to have.

Was it you who stole my bicycle?
        Where did you go?
                Where did all the chickens come from?

My bicycle is leaning up against the railings by the entrance
to the restaurant, looking fat, and the rain is yellow.

                        What have you done with all the chickens?

You know, I've never driven tractors, even if I often wanted to.

Perhaps I need the sunshine in the morning, recharging alkalines,
fertilising next year's crops. The conversation slowed.
The chickens were with the gold at the furthest outer limits of the
    rainbow.

# Pond life

The hosepipe has been banned from the garden.
I water my house.  The wallpaper is blooming
but the wood-fuelled stove has died.

On the mantelpiece a horse is asking me for words
but I keep on only making sounds of horses –
read this book I say. James Joyce, it's good for you.

What will we do when the summer turns to spring?
Waiting at the bus stop with a paper underneath our arms
and knee-length mackintoshes in preparation for the day?

They say it's an apocalypse but we'll take the chance –
dancing on the graves of apple groves and holding hands.
Yesterday is just a day ago but we're leaving it already.

Let's take the spaceship to the sky where there is orange
blossom, hosepipes, books, and horses cannot read.
The seed of sunflower is to broach the water's edge.

## Without feet

a month already so much sky

*apus apus* swoop the swifts
as they navigate their patterns
around my limestone skull

this repeated summer –
aerial crosses navigating blue
at the join of sea to sky

i am restless as a listening rock
i am opened like a restless cave

watch the patterns of our voices
and the silent speed of speed
across my neck

*apus apus*

there had already been a million
moons of flight still flying

## Cutting up the heat of glaciers

Beyond the road,
the daily sense of blinking water,
awake despite ourselves.

We spent the morning indoors
workshopping planetary dead ends:
could we climb this one?
How did the last one begin?

A washed-up pier. The first man
and the first woman are left to grow
in the purposeless heat.

Constellations of paperweights,
sea ice – which should not have
been possible – liquid fossil clocks
seen from the angle of the sun.

Our focus held the concentration
of anniversaries, burning years.
Take these bits of aeroplane,
traffic cone and secondhand whale.
A preference for averages
risking routines of change.

Whose house were we really in?

We decide to build it here,
before we can catch hold of
anything more wonderful.

Submerge our globes in little alchemy,
mouthfuls collapsing into tables,
doll's head trucks passed by, by music,
eyes I thought we had put out.

Every day is a beautiful day,
we hoped, the scale of windows.

The more we looked,
The more it simply wasn't there

## The average spelling of the weather

Craving angles, we found
ourselves within a constant
lean of curves

>out of sight horizons
>if we only walk a little
>further

we walked a horse shoe
top to bottom, on its side

>letting luck from left
>to right

>stabilising openings
>into circles, tangents,
>two degrees

it was a tale of increments

>the concentration of
>the parts of each notation
>on the page

>what then?

The people kept their heads low, watched the road and kept on
walking.

## At the altar

The windows of the glassmaking
factories were blown with stones,
asbestos flaked the edges of the air
– the touch of atmospheric chemistry.

The altar's arches had collapsed into
the road and its cemetery was dead
while the woman in the unmarked
grocery was spider-webbed with dust.

I pulled the beaded curtains to the sky.
Look at the crumbling chimneys forming
at the edges of my eyes like sleep!
Even the wind was a shade of grey.

There were once the Gauls who
taught the monks who taught the Jews
the art of shaping molten quartz.
A way of seeing – through things.

But I could only stay a moment.
The nearby motorway cut a two-mile
hole in the Napoleonic mountainside.
The Roman road was grazed by sheep.

This is the way to the sea, they say;
the past which cut the present, future
footprints smeared on unblown glass.

# *Icarus*

*i.*

It's a warmer world
the closer that you fly
towards the sun

      We're backing into knowledge
          hanging on it
             our wings
    around our necks like clews
    and our noses to the sky

We took the route untravelled
and unravelled it
      strings of daylight tangling
round our fingers just like flax

    What had we started.

        Climbing contours higher
          splitting rungs
       of atmospheric gases

    sculpting skies from uncompleted
    spaces bound in wax

*ii.*

Just working models
      otherwise applied –

      the reflections
of the whites of our eyes

      encircling what?

The heat of globes.
The way we talk about it.


*iii.*


I didn't think it would be blue
inside the sun

   I'd brought a saw and a set square
     sliced a geometric corner
  from the edges of its flames

     reassigning claims –
       to what?

Metaphors which open
into dissolution
   The colour of pupils

     Take another breath
     and hold yourself to it

      pin it to the light

# Notes

**'Variations on an urban monotone', xxv, 'Oranges'**
*jesus is a lesbian upon a beach in donegal* is the title of an artwork by Lisa Fingleton.

**'Fountainbridge'**
*Adele 19* is the title of an album by the singer Adele.

**'Herring boats'**
The words in italics are quotations from the architect of the Scottish parliament building, Enric Miralles.

**'Schiehallion'**
'The mountains are calling me and I must go' is a quotation from the Scottish-born writer and naturalist John Muir.